Meditation
★
The Science and Art
of Stillness

by
Nayaswami Vijay
(Lawrence Vijay Girard)

FruitgardenPublishing
"Information and Inspiration
for Living in Harmony with Life"

First Printing 2010

ISBN 0-9646457-7-7
EAN-13: 9780964645776
Printed in the United States of America

To all the great souls who have kept
the practice of meditation alive
through the millieum.

To Paramhansa Yogananda who
brought Hong-Sau and Kriya Yoga to
the West.

To Adi Nayaswami Kriyananda who
has inspired my life and meditations.

Contents

Introduction

It was early in 1964 that Beatlemania swept across America. Like every other American I had no idea of the part that the Beatles would play in shepherding in a new era of music. Who would have guessed that their unique music and hair style would coincide with the modern widespread introduction of meditation to the western world? I certainly couldn't have anticipated that my own life would be touched by that turn of events.

When the world heard that the Beatles were practicing Transcendental Meditation it caused an international stir. The news swept across America with the same faddish power as lava lamps, the peace sign and fallout shelters.

Suddenly, along with the changing of consciousness through the use of recreational drugs and the sexual revolution, there was an unexpected connection to the ancient tradition of meditation that had been handed down, generation after generation, for thousands of years by yogis in India. One evening I found myself at a lecture promoting the value of meditation and the next thing I knew our whole family was being initiated into Transcendental Meditation. It was 1967 and I was 15 years old.

Meditation: The Science and Art of Stillness

Attending a short private ceremony that took place in the bedroom of a home in Hollywood, California, I sat on the floor with an orange robed man in front of a small table which made due as an altar. The man giving me initiation chanted some words in Sanskrit and waved a stick of incense. Then he turned to me and pronounced some strange syllables that were to become my mantra. It seemed a little odd to me at the time that I felt no connection to this person or had little understanding of what was taking place; yet I felt calm and open.

After the ceremony I was sent into another room to sit alone and repeat the mantra mentally while sitting cross-legged on the floor. I sat in meditation not really knowing what I was supposed to do besides repeating the mantra mentally. Would anything happen? After a while it didn't seem so. I got up to rejoin my family.

On my way to the living room where the others were waiting the woman who was hosting the initiations in her home asked me how it went. I didn't immediately respond, I just stared at her, feeling like she was speaking to me from a great distance. After looking into my eyes and pausing for a moment she then said, "I see that you went deep. That's good."

At the time I had no idea what she was talking about. Only years later did I realize that I had experienced some of the deep calmness that comes from meditation. And that it can take the mind some time after experiencing inner peace to come back out for daily interactions. Even more importantly, I later learned that the way to evaluate the effectiveness of meditation isn't only during its practice, but by watching the affect it has on our lives when we are not meditating.

I practiced the TM meditation technique on and off for a few months. I felt calmer when I practiced but at that time of my life…excitement was more to my liking! It was only at the grand old age of 17 that I began to realize that inner stillness was to be valued more highly than outward stimulation. This understanding was made clear to me when I read a life changing book.

When I first saw the cover of the Beatles album, Sgt. Pepper's Lonely Hearts Club Band, I looked without recognition at the pictures of Mahavatar Babaji, Lahiri Mahasaya, Swami Sri Yukteswar and Paramhansa Yogananda, who are the Self-Realization line of Gurus that I was to discover when I read Yogananda's book, *Autobiography of a Yogi*, in the summer of 1969. After reading *Autobiography of a Yogi* suddenly life in general and meditation in particular made sense. I discovered that yoga meditation techniques are a science and not a set of hocus pocus beliefs. Through the science of yoga meditation we can access our inner potential of peace, joy, calmness, creativity and love.

Like many others, I was surprised to find out that you don't need to believe in God or even associate meditation with spirituality. As a purely mental and physiological process meditation reduces stress, which leads to improved mental and physical well-being. This has been studied extensively by qualified scientists. Still, there will always be a few grumblers in the back row who disagree. Most people in medicine and the general public accept that meditation is beneficial. While one might also consider the idea that it is unlikely something would be handed down generation after generation for over 5,000 years if it didn't work, one of the most basic tenants of yoga is: Don't take anyone's word for it! Experiment in the laboratory of your own life and experience truth directly.

The practical truth is that a person of any background or set of beliefs - as long as those beliefs don't keep a person

Meditation: The Science and Art of Stillness

from actually trying meditation - can improve the quality of their life if they just add the practice of meditation to their daily routine. Because meditation is based on science and not belief every practitioner will attain some benefit. At the same time, as with all things in life, some people will find meditation easier than others. There are a variety of factors that will affect each person's practice. Dedicated application of the techniques is essential. You can't say it doesn't work if you don't actually practice the techniques!

There is also the issue of support while you get started. Like my early efforts with TM, if I had support during that time I might have stayed with it, but I was on my own and none of my friends were even remotely interested in meditation. If there is one thing that I would say to most people in order to increase their chances of success with meditation, it would be to find a place for regular group practice. It was only after I found an environment that supported meditation that my own practice dramatically improved. If we think about it, this is true with most endeavors in life. The group energy of others, going in the same direction we want to go, is almost always beneficial. For many people, it is essential.

The techniques that I will be sharing in this book have been taught to me by Nayaswami Kriyananda, a direct disciple of Paramhansa Yogananda. I myself became a disciple of Paramhansa Yogananda in 1969 and have been associated with Nayaswami Kriyananda since 1972. I mention this tradition because the fact is that the word meditation means different things to different people. While there are many good sources for basic meditation techniques it is important to understand that all teachers don't teach the same thing.

I should mention here that it is a mistake to try and learn advanced meditation techniques only from a book. Advanced meditation techniques should be learned directly from an experienced practitioner who will also provide pre and post ongoing support. If you have a choice I recommend learning a beginning meditation technique in person as well, but in the case of a beginner, a book or video is better than nothing!

Many meditation teachers today mix and match ideas and techniques that they have read all under the heading of meditation. While I would say that it is all generally beneficial, that doesn't mean that it is all equally beneficial. A charismatic teacher alone doesn't guarantee the quality of a technique. And not all techniques are equally effective. One of the best ways to gauge the quality of a teaching is to meet people who have practiced it for an extended period of time. When meeting such a person ask yourself: How does this person feel? Are they calm? Peaceful? Joyful? Do they represent the kind of person I want to become?

If you find a group of people who are practicing the same technique and they feel like "your kind of people" then that is a positive sign that the technique they practice will be good for you.

While it is true that yoga meditation is a science, it is also an art. Each yogi (yoga practitioner) will find their own unique way to blend and live the many facets of yoga practice. This is what keeps the science alive and fresh. Each of us can take this ancient practice and experience its central truths in our own unique way.

The goal of Yoga Practice is the state of Satchidananda - ever-existing, ever-conscious, ever-new joy. Each of us has the potential to achieve this state if we apply ourselves with sufficient diligence. If your goal is more modest, like reducing stress and maybe experiencing a little peace, you can certainly do

Meditation: The Science and Art of Stillness

this. Don't be intimidated by ultimate goals. You don't have to scale Mount Everest to gain the benefits of hiking. At the same time, if you do aspire to the top of any field in life, meditation can help you get there. If you also want to experience life's central truth of universal love and joy, meditation is a must.

It is my great joy to pass on to you these techniques that have been of such great benefit in my own life. They have proven through the millennium to work. It is my hope that you also will join with others in the sacred practice of meditation. It is science, it is art, it is the path to life's central truth of oneness.

Namaste - Spirit in me bows to the Spirit in you.

Chapter 1
Why Meditation?

Why meditation?

The answer to this is so simple, yet deeply profound, that it is easy for many people to not believe that it could be true.

Meditation is the most direct way to experience true and lasting happiness.

It still amazes me that so many of the truths of life hide right in front of us but we close our eyes to them and shout: It can't be known!

This is how life works.

Take about one thousand reasonably intelligent people. Ask them: Where can happiness be found? Most of them will reply after some thought: Happiness is to be found within! This is common knowledge. Yet if you look at the lives of those 1,000 people you will find that maybe one is looking within and all the rest are looking outside themselves in outward experiences or possessions for happiness.

Meditation: The Science and Art of Stillness

Multiply this thousand people until it equals the population of planet earth and you now understand what is going on in this world. The majority of people are looking outside of themselves for a happiness that they can only find within themselves.

Meditation is central to experiencing happiness on the inside instead of seeking false happiness on the outside.

Let me explain what I mean by false happiness.

The confusion starts from the time we are born. We find ourselves in a body that instinctively seeks pleasure and learns to avoid pain. In the beginning pleasures are simple: we eat, sleep and poop. We enjoy a good hug. We respond to life with a laugh or a cry as the most basic emotional responses. As we grow we engage ourselves with the exploration of interests in the world around us.

Most people follow the simple guideline of embracing pleasure and avoiding pain. Each of us develops preferences that add personal definition to what pleasure and pain mean to us. Thus everyone creates an intricate web of characteristics that becomes their self-definition. This self-definition is the sum total of reactions to the environment of life in which we have lived. Most people live on a seesaw that tips between that which they like and that which they do not like. This is how the outside world takes control over our ability to be happy.

Does this tell the whole story? Not exactly.

You see, all of this conditioning has convinced us that happiness is when we are experiencing pleasure. We know that pleasure isn't the same for everyone because not everyone likes the same things. Many people take great pleasure in riding a roller coaster or climbing a mountain. While others would consider those activities to be torture. Some people take enjoyment eating foods that others couldn't force themselves to put in their own mouth. It becomes quickly clear that people don't feel the same about everything. As the saying goes: One man's pleasure is another man's pain.

So far, we can see that people are seeking their own form of happiness through the things that they personally enjoy. Since the majority of people approach life this way we may be hesitant to stand outside of the mainstream and ask this most obvious question: Does this approach to life actually work?

If we look at the lives of the rich and famous who have the wherewithal to surround themselves with the things they enjoy we find that they are not guaranteed happiness. The media is daily filled with their suffering producing escapades. A number of studies have shown that people with money, fame and outward success are just as likely to commit suicide as poor people.

On the other end of the spectrum we might consider people who live simple lives out in the country. Are they happier? While they enjoy the benefits of life in the country they still get sick, have accidents and have to pay taxes. Certainly in many cases their lives are simpler. Simplicity in itself avoids many of the complexities of life that often lead to unpleasant problems. But is this by itself the same as dynamic happiness? In fact, we might even ask: Is dynamic lasting happiness even possible?

We can see that happiness isn't in things themselves. If it were everyone would like the same things or be happy with the things they have. Is there something that makes everyone happy? What is happiness?

Meditation: The Science and Art of Stillness

The answers to these essential questions are found all around us in the way that people of all races and nations are made. No matter what the outward circumstances of any people they all experience love, peace and joy that emanates spontaneously from within. We all know this and experience it even though we don't quite understand it.

I am not talking about the highs and lows of the emotions. I am talking about the deep well of positive feelings that we occasionally recognize inside ourselves when we are feeling good about life. Most people are so distracted by the world outside themselves that they are only vaguely aware that this is where happiness comes from. The idea that we can consciously connect to this inner point of happiness and increase our experience of well-being without needing outward stimulus is, if not outright unthinkable, definitely not consistent with the pervasive lifestyle of consumerism.

Let me ask you. Where do you experience love?

Everyone knows that we experience love in the heart. I have never heard of a person saying that they experience love in their neck, back or leg. This is a universal experience that is only up to debate with the people who still think the world is flat.

Is there a difference between universal love and human love? Yes.

Most human experiences are based in the emotions. Emotions by their nature cause an up or a down in the mental landscape. First we are happy and then we are sad. In human love we find that it keeps close company with its counterpart: hate. Thus you find couples that vow to "love each other forever" and then "hate each other forever" across the table in divorce court.

Love that is rooted in universal love has no ups and downs. It is always calm and at rest unto itself. Extended from a deep inner wellspring, this kind of love is never withdrawn and is not subject to the fluctuations of daily life. Universally connected love is so dynamic and all encompassing that it is called Divine. True Divine love is not bound by religion or any other set of beliefs. It is a universal truth that all can experience directly through the scientific practice of meditation.

Universal consciousness has eight main manifestations: light, sound, power, peace, joy, calmness, wisdom and love. These are the main components of the eternal ocean of happiness potential that we can all access if we practice meditation. Yoga (Union) with universal consciousness is called Samadhi - conscious oneness. Yoga practice doesn't require labeling this consciousness with words like God, Life, Nature or any other name.

Yoga says: Be a true scientist. Reach past belief and doubt. Experiment within the laboratory of your own consciousness to experience on the deepest level the most basic truth; that happiness is found within.

Chapter 2
What is Meditation?

Sometimes people misunderstand each other simply because the words they use mean different things to different people. Let me begin by explaining what it does not mean, from a yoga teachings point of view, to meditate.

Meditation is not making the mind blank; yogis do not seek emptiness or nothingness. In fact it is just the opposite. Eventually the yogi becomes one with "everythingness".

Meditation is not listening to some nice soft music while a soothing voice describes pleasant and uplifting thoughts. I would describe this as a visualization; nice, useful, sometimes a good preparation for meditation, but not in itself the same as meditation.

Occasionally you hear people say they were meditating over a problem. What they usually mean – unless they are familiar with yoga meditation - is that they were mulling it over in their mind and maybe trying to opening themselves up to new ideas. This type of open thinking is useful, but not the same as the process we will be exploring.

Yoga meditation is not walking out into the forest or

down to the beach and letting your mind reach out into nature. Nor is it a walking meditation or mindfulness, where you walk slowly and calmly with conscious intent to be fully aware of the moment. These are both excellent practices that I can recommend highly, but they are not yoga meditation as we will be discussing it.

Biofeedback techniques are not the same as yoga meditation.

In order to understand what yoga meditation actually is, it will be helpful to understand clearly what we are trying to accomplish when we meditate. Let's start by exploring how the mind works.

The Three Aspects of the Mind

There are three aspects to the mind: the conscious mind, the subconscious mind and the superconscious mind.

The conscious mind is where we live most of the time. This is the workstation where we take in new information, make decisions and guide our lives. The conscious mind animates the body and personality in such a way as to give the impression that we and the body/personality are one and the same. This is a false impression, but in order to explain how this is so we need to review the subconscious mind.

The subconscious mind is the repository of our memories. It is also the storehouse of our likes and dislikes, our habits and the various components that make up our personality. It drives the automatic processes of the body and holds a powerful sway over the conscious mind. It is in the subconscious mind that we usually wander during dreamtime.

What is Meditation?

The conscious and subconscious mind work in tandem, giving the impression that they alone are responsible for our awareness. By centering our awareness in the conscious and subconscious mind we accept that we are alone and separate from all others. This is the ego. The ego is like a costume that is worn on the outside but someone else is inside. Who is inside? Well, that is the soul. The ego is the soul identified with the body. The soul is our connection to the superconscious mind.

I am trying to simplify something that would take volumes to explain completely. Do you need to agree with or believe any of this explanation to practice and receive the benefits of meditation? No. But this explanation can help you to understand what this "happiness within us" is all about. And that can help you to visualize what is trying to happen when we meditate - which will then make it easier to harmonize with the process.

The superconscious mind is the soul's connection to infinite potential and happiness. When we are connected to the superconscious mind we can begin to access ever greater amounts of energy, creative ideas, joy and love. The goal is that we live centered in the superconscious mind, which would then activate the conscious and subconscious minds from a much higher octave. When we live this way we will experience inner calmness and contentment no matter what happens in outward life. This means not only a little stress reduction, but also oneness with all life and freedom from the delusion of ego and death.

Why aren't we aware of the superconscious mind already?

Well - and this is the real rub - most people are aware of it to some degree but we have chosen to ignore it. The

Meditation: The Science and Art of Stillness

superconscious mind touches us when we feel uplifted, when we love on a deeper level than emotion, when we access a new positive creative idea and when we feel the joy of service to others. Many people have superconscious dreams in which they receive new ideas and life guidance. Intuitive perception – which is the way the superconscious mind works – is often dismissed as a lucky hunch or a coincidence. A common example of intuition is the subtle connection that mothers have with their children. All positive qualities in life are linked to some degree in the superconscious mind.

There are many powerful forces in life that are at work underneath the surface of our perceptions. Yogis of ancient times explored these forces. Instead of directing their inquiries outwardly into nature like modern scientists, they turned the power of the mind inwardly to explore their own inner selves.

Here, in a nutshell, is the classic description of what those sages discovered.

The mind is like the surface of the ocean. When the ocean is calm it perfectly reflects the moonlight. But when it is disturbed by a storm the light becomes fragmented and appears to be many lights rather than just one. Thus the mind, disturbed by the countless inputs of outward existence, becomes restlessness and unable to reflect perfectly the superconscious peace of infinite Spirit.

Meditation

Meditation is the process of stilling the mind so that it can once again reflect perfectly its natural state of superconscious perception.

When we meditate we are gradually shifting our

center of awareness from the conscious/subconscious mind to the superconscious mind. It is this process of redirecting our awareness from the lower to the higher that we engage in during meditation. This is a very specific act that is guided by the way that we are made.

Paramhansa Yogananda defined meditation as: The single pointed focusing of the mind on a specific technique or aspect of God.

Here is how it works.

The ancient sages discovered that there is a subtle link between the mind and the breath. We can observe this in our own lives. When we are very concentrated the breath is calm. When the mind is agitated the breath is very active and restless. This connection between the mind and breath is used to make meditation highly effective.

Try this experiment.

Take a moment and close your eyes - after you read what to do! With your eyes closed take a look at your current level of calmness or restlessness. Just take a quick look at how you feel. Then open your eyes and keep reading.

Now that you have taken a mental inventory of how you feel inwardly I want you to inhale with a deep breath through your nose. Hold for the count of three. And then exhale through your mouth. Do this once more. Inhale deeply through the nose, hold for the count of three and then exhale through the mouth.

Close your eyes again and see how you feel now.

Meditation: The Science and Art of Stillness

Most people will find that they have just experienced a noticeable change in their level of awareness. They feel calmer, more inwardly connected and more focused.

All we did was take two conscious breaths and suddenly our inner weather is completely different. I can only assume that you were breathing normally before trying this experiment. You have taken countless breaths without this result. The reason these two breaths have such a dramatic effect is because they were taken with conscious intent.

This is called Pranayama (life/breath/energy control). The use of the breath to control and direct our inner energy is key to attaining stillness of mind. It is only in stillness that we can fully receive our potential for inner joy and guidance.

I mention guidance here because many people don't realize that the universe is our friend. If you learn to calm your mind and then ask the universe a question you will receive an answer. It probably won't be a voice from the heavens! With practice you will discover the subtle – and sometime not so subtle! - hand of the universal presence participating in your life.

Mantra

Along with controlling or not controlling the breath, according to the guidelines of any specific meditation technique, many techniques use a mantra. A mantra is a word or words that have specific meaning and vibrational content that are beneficial for the attainment of one's goals. Mantras are usually repeated mentally only and not with the voice. Not all meditation techniques use a mantra. Most often mantras are Sanskrit - which is considered by yogis to be vibrationally superior to other languages.

Magnetism

The subject of energy, vibration and magnetism might seem unconnected to meditation, but that couldn't be farther from the truth. Science tells us that all of life is energy and that all energy puts out a magnetic field. This field can attract or repulse other energies according to its polarity. Yogis see the spine in the human body as a magnet with the negative polarity at the base of the spine and the positive polarity in the brain. Yogis have understood that meditation has a powerful effect on this magnetism.

Universal Consciousness

Scientists in the exploration of Quantum Physics have discovered outwardly what Yogis discovered inwardly thousands of years ago, which is that underlying all energy in the creation is consciousness. All of life is one infinite consciousness. This scientific revelation is the beginning of the dissolution of the gap between science and spirituality. The way to experience our own unique connection to this infinite consciousness fully is through meditation.

By turning the mind inward upon itself in meditation and calming the storm of restless thoughts that cloud our inner perception we can discover for ourselves the inner universe of happiness that is at the very core of all life.

Chapter 3
Is Meditation Science or Religion?

One of the quirks of Western thought is that everything in life should be either this or that, black or white, good or bad. In Eastern thought there is a different approach. Yogis see truth like a diamond with many facets; each facet has its own unique beauty, but is also part of the whole. It simply isn't possible to encompass infinite truth with a single point of view, unless that view is at the very center and able to perceive all views simultaneously. Achieving this center view, a universal view or God's view, is the inevitable result of perfect meditation.

Is meditation science? Is meditation religion? It is neither and it is both. Let me explain.

First, let's review the basis of science. Scientists take a hypothesis and verify its truth with an experiment. If that experiment produces the expected result and can be duplicated by other scientists then the hypothesis is accepted as scientific fact.

According to this scientific method it has been proven that meditation lowers the heart rate and reduces blood pressure. This leads to the calming of the mind and muscle relaxation, thus achieving the reduction of stress. So far, meditation meets the basic requirement of science, that the same result can be reproduced by anyone replicating the experiment.

At the same time, to describe the only usefulness of meditation as a prescription for stress reduction is like getting into a formula one race car and driving it at twenty-five miles an hour to get groceries. The usage in both cases, while being truly useful, doesn't begin to utilize the full capabilities of either vehicle.

The thing to understand about this is that science can prove that the race car will travel at over 200 miles per hour. But as a practical matter, not everyone is capable or even interested in doing their own experiment to see if they can drive the car that fast. It takes training, determination and practice. It is the same with meditation.

Almost anyone can get a little peace through meditation. We just got a taste of it by simply taking two conscious breaths! But to fully access the potential of meditation it takes an extended period of training and dedication.

The reason the question of religion presents itself is that throughout history men and women who have dedicated themselves to years of long and deep meditation have had such extraordinary results that their accomplishments have transcended "scientific belief" and entered the realm of the "miraculous".

Much more important than seemingly impossible feats like not breathing and not eating for extended periods of time, or appearing in more than one body simultaneously in two places, are the lives of these great souls who inspire and heal others through the depth of their joy, love and compassion. The challenge for many people is to believe what has actually been proven to be true; and most importantly, to believe that which you can prove for yourself. For what difference does it make if we have a higher potential if we aren't interested in seeking it?

Most religions are a set of beliefs that one is expected to accept without personal verification. You just have to have faith! I am not suggesting that people should not believe. I am saying that you can be more scientific in your religion by going past belief to actual experience. It isn't enough to simply say, "I believe in God." We should go on to actually experience God's presence in our lives.

God by definition is omnipresent. So why can't we see Him/Her? Simply put, our minds are so restless that we can't perceive that which is always present. Meditation, stilling the mind, is the way to prove through an experiment in your own consciousness the hypothesis of God's existence.

As I mentioned earlier, yoga practice does not require a belief in God or Universal Consciousness. Yoga is not a set of beliefs, it is a practice that leads of its own accord to direct knowledge of that which is most centrally true in life.

True religion is not about what we believe, but how we actually live. Most people who claim religious affiliation don't actually worship God. They worship their own self-interests and desires: money, fame, social status, good looks and lastly if they believe in the afterlife, avoidance of hell after death. When they have problems they pray for help. Where are the souls that love God without asking for anything in return?

The things we think about most become that which we worship. Those who aspire to a religious life want not just to think about God but to actually commune with God in deep meditation. The religions of the world can be seen as facets

Meditation: The Science and Art of Stillness

of the Divine gem. Each path represents a beautifully unique expression of Spirit. It is only though communion with infinite Spirit that the religions of the world can be vitalized and renewed with each successive generation.

The disconnection between spirituality and religion can be seen in the disunity that has presented itself all around the world. There is no true religion that preaches hate. Yet followers of many religions practice intolerance to the point of violence. Then people with common sense look at religion and for good reason doubt that religion is what it claims to be: the path of love, peace and compassion.

Religious orders around the world are doing many good works, but by-in-large they have left communion with God to the prophets of old. If you want to truly understand the bridge between science and religion you must cultivate within your own heart a dynamic relationship with Life, God, the Universe. One of the most powerful ways you can do this is through meditation.

Chapter 4
Preparation for Meditation

Just like getting ready for any important event in life, we need to prepare ourselves for meditation. Swami Kriyananda said, "Meditation is the oil that keeps the machinery of life running smoothly." Once you have established a regular meditation practice you will wonder how you ever got along without it.

In this chapter we will discuss a number of skills and tips that will be linked in the next chapter to meditation practice. As with many activities in life, once you become adept you can skip or adjust your preparation routine as you please. In the beginning though, these steps are like preparing the soil in the garden for the planting of seeds; the better the preparation the greater the chances of a good harvest.

The preparation of body, mind and spirit for meditation takes place all at the same time. Even though out of necessity I will present these items in a linear fashion, keep in mind that they are all connect and should be applied as appropriate at all times. As with any type of exercise, only you can determine how to apply the exercises in a way that doesn't cause any physical injury to your body, so while I encourage you to be enthusiastic, don't injure yourself!

Meditation: The Science and Art of Stillness
Proper Breathing

That most of us were not trained at a young age about proper breathing is one of the great educational mysteries. The average person takes over 17,000 breaths per day. Yet most people, unless they have had musical training for singing or playing a wind instrument, don't realize that we limit our ability to inhale fully when we walk around with our stomachs sucked in or bound by tight fitting clothes. In order to completely fill the lungs it is necessary for the abdominal muscles to relax so that the lungs can inflate downward – since they are restricted above and to the sides by the limitations of the rib cage. If we don't relax the abdominal muscles we will restrict the amount of air that can enter the lungs.

Prana is the Sanskrit word for life, breath and energy. The ancient seers use of one word to describe all three tells us that our preconception that they are separate is incorrect . The deeper meaning of Prana is life force. The more you have of life force the more alive you are. When the life force is withdrawn the body is dead. The reason people can be resuscitated after a heart attack is that their essential life force has not yet left the body. You can pump a dead body with air and zap it with electricity (energy) but if the life force has fully withdrawn the body will not re-animate. If this were not true then the creation of the Frankenstein monster would be possible. Through conscious breathing we draw upon more life force for mental, physical and spiritual well-being.

Here is how to check the way you breathe. You can do this sitting or standing, but it is easiest if you are lying down on your back.

Start by extending your spine so that it is as straight as possible. Then place one hand on your chest above the heart and the other hand on your abdomen above the navel. Without controlling your breath watch what your hands do while you breathe. Notice if they are going up, down or staying the same. Are there any differences in motion between inhalation and exhalation? Now take a deep breath and notice if there are any changes.

Now that you have taken a look at the way you breathe let's try something that may be new to you, it is called diaphragmatic breathing. Use the hand that is over your heart to monitor your chest. Take a slow deep breath but don't let your chest expand out. Make sure the hand on your chest stays at the same level and doesn't move. In order to fill your lungs you will need to relax your abdominal muscles so that the lungs can expand down. This will make you feel like you are poking your stomach out.

You will find that you can get more air into your lungs this way. If you doubt this, take a breath consciously holding your stomach muscles tense and see what happens. Your lungs feel the restriction of the rib cage. Relax the stomach muscles and take another deep breath. You will feel like your lungs were set free.

When you can feel the hand over your stomach rising and falling while the hand over your chest moves little or not at all, you are breathing correctly.

It is natural for the rib cage to expand during a deep breath but if the lungs don't fill down and out as well, lung capacity is unnecessarily limited. Unless directed otherwise, when practicing breathing exercises you should use this type of diaphragmatic breathing.

Meditation: The Science and Art of Stillness
The Full Yogic Breath

The full yogic breath exercise is used to draw energy into the body and to release mental and physical tension. We use the hands as magnets to sweep the energy up and down the body while inhaling and exhaling with a deep yogic breath. Start in a standing position with your hands at you sides.

- While you slowly inhale through the nose, imagine that your hands are magnets and bring them in a flowing motion - palms towards your body - side by side in front of your navel.

- Then sweep your hands up the front of your body and stretch them above your head as far as you can reach.

- Your inhalation should end when your hands reach the top above your head.

- Pause your breath for a moment and stretch up, you can even go up on your toes if you like.

- Now slowly exhale through the mouth as you sweep your palms down the front of your body.

- When you get to the navel begin to bend forward at the waist.

- Keeping your legs as straight as is comfortable, bend down until your hands sweep all the way down to the tips of your toes.

- When you reach the bottom extension your lungs should be as empty as possible.

- One round of this exercise is when you sweep the palms up the front of the body, stretch up and sweep the hands down to the feet again.

- Complete the exercise by staying upright - after the last inhalation, bring your hands back to rest at your sides while you exhale.

- Stand with your eyes closed for a few moments after the exercise. Breath normally and enjoy the both calming and vitalizing effect of the exercise.

When you practice the full yogic breath you will need to synchronize the flow of the breath with the speed of your sweeping motion so that your lungs are empty at the bottom and full at the top. Feel that you are inhaling energy, vitality and positivity into your body, mind and spirit as you sweep your hands up. Visualize that you are magnetically sweeping the energy in the spine with the hands. As you exhale and bend forward feel that you are releasing all mental, physical and spiritual tensions. Imagine all tensions being swept away by your magnetic hands and released into the earth beneath you.

Repeat this exercise 5 to 7 times. Be sure to use diaphragmatic breathing for a full breath. If you feel light-headed it means you are putting more oxygen into the body than it is used to. You should stop and do fewer repetitions next time until your body adjusts.

Asana and Hatha Yoga

Many people think that Asana (posture) is the same as Hatha Yoga (Yoga Postures), this is not exactly correct. Asana is the attainment of the ability to sit straight and still for extended

Meditation: The Science and Art of Stillness

hours of meditation. In order to prepare the body for this state of physical stillness the practices of Hatha Yoga were developed. When practiced as inward preparation for meditation Hatha Yoga leads naturally to physical and mental inner calmness. The physical health benefits are considered a secondary benefit.

While it is not necessary to practice Hatha Yoga in order to meditate it is immensely helpful - particularly for beginners. Ananda Yoga is a style of Hatha Yoga that Swami Kriyananda developed specifically to emphasize Yoga Postures as preparation for meditation. By giving particular attention to the rest points between the postures, inner focus, affirmations and deep relaxation – which includes the conscious withdrawal of energy from all the body parts - Ananda Yoga is the ideal way to prepare for meditation.

I refer you to AnandaYoga.Org for more information on Hatha Yoga practice.

Pranayama

Yama means control. So Pranayama means control of the life force. In order to do this we use the breath. There are many Pranayama techniques (breathing exercises), each designed for very specific results. We are now going to learn two techniques that will be very helpful as preparation for the Hong-Sau meditation technique - which we will discuss in the next chapter. You do not have to do these every time you practice the Hong-Sau meditation technique but it is recommended that you use them as a regular part of your practice.

Double Breathing with Tension

This is the first of a series of Energization Exercises that were developed by Paramhansa Yogananda. Yogananda explained that life force comes into the body through the Medulla Oblongata at the base of the brain. Normally it is distributed automatically through the spinal centers (Chakras) which then activate their counterparts in the physical body. Through the Energization Exercises we can learn to access and direct life force through the use of will power.

Here is how it works.

Make a fist and tense it as tight as you can. Now tense it tighter. Tighter! Tighter! Now relax the hand muscles and shake it out.

What just happened?

You used your will power to send energy down your arm to your hand. When you first tightened it you thought you had tensed it all the way. But then each time you tried you found that you could actually tense it more. This demonstrates how we do the Energization Exercises and also gives us an example of how the only limit to how much life force we can access is in the mind.

In Double Breathing with Tension we will tense and relax all of the muscles in the body simultaneously. It will take some time to mentally coordinate tensing all your muscles at the same time. While we do this we will inhale and exhale with what is called a double breath. The double breath is a short-long inhalation through the nose and a short-long exhalation through the mouth. So the air goes in-innnn through the nose and out-ouuut through the mouth.

It is helpful if you really exaggerate the sounds of the air flowing. It might sound a little silly, but it helps. The exhalation sounds like ha-haaa - the sound of the air going out

31

of the lungs, not a vocalization. I can't really describe the sound of the inhalation but it has the same short-long flow.

When you tense all of your body muscles, do so in a low-medium-high flow. So you will tense low-medium-high, hold for the count of three, and then relax high-medium-low relaxed. We will synchronize the breath so that we inhale and tense the muscles at the same time. Hold the breath and high muscle tension for the count of three. Then exhale while relaxing the muscles. As you tense all of the muscles in your body, your hands should form naturally into fists and then relax to an open palms up position on your thighs while the rest of the body relaxes.

So here is how we put it all together.

- Sit with your hands palms up comfortably on your thighs.

- Inhale through the nose with a double breath while you tense all the muscles in the body: low-medium-high.

- Hold the breath and maintain the muscles at high tension for the count of three.

- Exhale with the double breath through the mouth while relaxing the muscles: high-medium-low relaxed.

- During tension be sure to check and see if you have included all of your muscles, don't forget to include the face, neck, chest, back, abdomen and toes.

Preparation for Meditation

There are two important maxims that Paramhansa
Yogananda shared about practicing the Energization Exercises:

"The greater the will, the greater the flow of energy."

"Tense with will, relax and feel."

Keep these in mind as you practice this exercise.

There are several variations on how to do this exercise.
For our purpose I have assumed you are sitting for meditation.
It can also be done standing up or lying down if you want to try
it separately from meditation. Repeat the exercise 3 to 5 times.

While you do the exercise try to visualize the life force
animating the muscles and then withdrawing back to the brain.
In the beginning you will just feel like you are breathing and
tensing the muscles, but over time you will begin to feel the
subtle life force behind those physical actions. This conscious
on-off activation and conscious direction of life force is the
beginning of understanding what is taking place during the use
of advanced meditation techniques.

12-12-12 Breathing

This exercise is quite simple, but very effective. We are
going to inhale through the nose with a normal breath, hold,
and then exhale through the mouth. The key here is that the
inhalation, hold, and exhalation should all be equal in duration.
The length of the count depends on your current lung capacity
- longer is better, but you should not get out of breath. If you
find yourself out of breath you are using too many counts. So in
the beginning you might do 6-6-6, but over time you can work
your way up to 12-12-12 or longer. Again, the key is to go as
many counts as you can without getting out of breath between

rounds. One round is an inhalation, hold, and exhalation. For this example we will start with 6-6-6.

- Sitting in a relaxed upright posture, inhale through the nose to the count of 6.

- Hold the breath for the count of 6.

- Exhale through the mouth for the count of 6.

In the beginning I recommend you do 3 to 5 rounds. You can increase that to 5 to 7 rounds when you feel comfortable. Don't be in too much of a hurry! Quality is better than quantity.

Right Attitude

I can't emphasize enough how important right attitude is throughout your practice of meditation. It starts before you sit to meditate but also carries through to one's attitude during and after meditation. In the West we are raised on the achievement of goals. This frame of mind can be very helpful in life, but in meditation it can be a detriment. I would offer that the goal of sitting to meditate regularly is the only place that we should apply pressure on ourselves - for without regular practice little progress can be expected. The rest of our meditation practice should be left un-judged and without expectation of results.

I am not suggesting that we don't mentally gauge how we are doing to some degree, but the fact is that in the beginning we don't actually have the experience to evaluate how we are doing. Yes, we will be able to tell that one session is calmer than another or that our inner focus seemed to be stronger or weaker. But keep in mind that great athletes are not made only on their good days, they are made on the many more days that things didn't go well but they kept on trying.

Preparation for Meditation

Just by doing any meditation practice at all you will find yourself becoming calmer. We have experienced this already with just a couple of breathing exercises! To reap the deeper life transforming benefits of meditation it will take participation over an extended period of time.

At the same time, we shouldn't take a laissez-faire attitude towards meditation. We should apply ourselves with focus of will, but not to the point that we create unnecessary tension. If you are anxious about your efforts, back off a little.

As best you can, leave your problems outside the door of your meditation space. There is a time to bring them into the meditation room, but only after you have become calm and inwardly connected. When you first sit to meditate imagine that you are going to dip your inner spirit into a pool of calmness. If you make a habit of bringing agitation into the meditation room it will be like a troublesome fly buzzing around your head, distracting you from your purpose.

You might say that if you could shed your problems easily you wouldn't need meditation! But I assure you, all but the most unpleasant of life experiences can be hung on the coat rack outside for a few minutes while you meditate. If you really can't, then of course bring them in. Over time you will find that with a little mental application you will be able to suspend even your greatest challenges for a time so that you can best prepare your mind and spirit to face them with equanimity.

More Preparation Tips

• Try not to eat before meditation. The heavier a meal, the longer you should wait before meditating. Thirty minutes to two hours is a general guideline. At the same time, it is better to meditate with a full stomach then to not meditate at all! It won't hurt you. It just makes sense that if your body is digesting food it won't want to withdraw that energy into the spine so you can merge with infinite joy!

• Avoid at all times recreational drugs. These drugs have negative residual effects on the mind for months – and sometimes years - after usage. Replace these activities with the natural high of meditation.

• Although yogis recommend abstinence from alcohol, an occasional drink won't incapacitate all of your efforts. But any regular drinking of alcohol will slow you down. If you are really serious about your meditation practice don't drink any alcohol. The good news is that the more you meditate, the less you will want to drink things that cloud your inner happiness.

• When possible, wash your body so it feels fresh.

• Wear loose clothing that doesn't impede your breathing.

• If you can, wear clothing that you only use for meditation. Of course this isn't always practical, but when possible, do so.

• Turn off your cell phone! And any other communication devices that might interrupt your meditation session.

Chapter 5
The Hong-Sau Meditation Technique

Many people think that the times we live in are amazing because of all the technological advances that have taken place in the last 100 years or so. I propose that the greatest blessing of our time is that advanced meditation techniques have been made readily available to the common man. Until fairly recently in India the Hong-Sau Meditation Technique was given to an applicant only after years of arduous preparation: today it is given to beginners. Many souls have achieved self-realization through this technique. If you apply it with diligence you can experience the truth of this statement in your own life.

Receiving this technique with an attitude of gratitude and practicing it with knowledge of the respect it deserves will go a long way to helping you practice it successfully. This is no toy, it is a sacred key that can open the door to what Yogananda described as "Undreamed of Possibilities."

Although the Hong-Sau Meditation Technique fits under the heading of "meditation techniques" Paramhansa Yogananda called it the "Hong-Sau Technique of Concentration." The use of the word concentration helps us to understand that meditation isn't the passive wandering of the mind. Until we can concentrate inwardly with complete focus we can't really

Meditation: The Science and Art of Stillness

say that we are actually meditating. So for quite some time we will be "trying to meditate" while we are meditating. This doesn't mean we won't get some positive results immediately, but it does give a realistic view of the beginner's circumstances.

Anyone who has tried to meditate will tell you how difficult it is to still the mind. As soon as you sit to meditate ideas about other activities, plans for the future and numerous disconnected thoughts will all appear frantically vying for your attention. Once you latch on to one of these thoughts it will take you to another, and another, endlessly until you notice what has happened. The Hong-Sau Technique is designed specifically to deal with this situation. When you are successfully practicing the technique you will be so focused on the technique that you simply won't notice if those thoughts are still around or not.

How to Sit for Meditation

We have discussed the meaning of Asana and how it represents the goal of being able to sit in meditation for extended periods. Yoga Postures were designed as a preparation for meditation, but there is one pose that is considered the best for meditation: the Lotus Pose. Unfortunately this pose is only for those with very limber legs. The good news is that by understanding the Lotus Pose we can easily duplicate the most important parts of the position.

Padmasana – the Lotus Pose

In the Lotus Pose the yogi sits cross-legged with the soles of the feet turned upward on the thigh of the opposite leg. In order to do this the bent left leg is placed on the right thigh and then the bent right leg is lifted up over the left calf in order to lock the legs in position. It is considered more correct to have the right calf on top of the left calf - the right side of the body is considered to have positive polarity. Though I would say that if you can sit with either foot on top…more power to you!

The overwhelmingly important part of the Lotus Pose is that it holds the spine straight. Yogananda said about the spine, "The spine is the highway to the Infinite." The reason the spine needs to be straight is so that Prana can flow up and down the spine without impediment. This straightness of the spine also allows for proper yogic breathing. The crossing and locking of the legs creates a strong and balanced base so the yogi won't easily fall over. Another benefit to this pose is that the hips are drawn into an optimal position for supporting the spine. We can see from this description that the most important parts of the Lotus Pose are: straight spine, hips properly positioned under the spine and balanced base.

Now we are going to explore ways to achieve these goals without actually sitting in the Lotus Pose – since it simply isn't practical for most people. All of the sitting options below will provide these prerequisites, though if you can comfortably use the Lotus Pose then do so. There are several cross-legged sitting positions besides the Lotus Pose, I recommend that you explore these with the general study of Hatha Yoga.

Sitting Cross-legged

There are numerous variations on this theme in Hatha Yoga. The basic idea is that you sit with crossed legs any way that feels comfortable to you. Experiment with folding your legs and tucking your feet into different positions until you find one that works for your body.

You can also sit on a pillow with your legs crossed in front. There are pillows designed for meditation that you can purchase or you can use a pillow that you already have.

Meditation: The Science and Art of Stillness

If you prefer sitting without a pillow, I recommend the use of a small rolled towel or blanket to be placed under the base of your spine or the edge of your rear end so that your hips are tucked comfortably underneath your spine. Experiment until you find the position that feels most comfortable to your body.

Vajrasana - the Firm Pose

This is a kneeling pose where you place your knees together on the floor and sit down on your calves and heels. This can be a very comfortable position if your body is not too large. It provides excellent spinal support. Even still, not many people can sit this way for an extended period of time. If you like this position I recommend you get a kneeling meditation bench that slides in between your calves and rear end. The bench takes the stretch and weight off your legs so you can sit longer.

Sitting in a chair

This is certainly the way most people can sit for an extended length of time. The keys to using a chair are that you don't lean back, the seat should be padded or pillowed to your comfort and it should be at a height that allows your feet to comfortably reach flat on the floor. You can use a small rolled towel, blanket or pillow to support the base of your spine in just the same way people sitting with crossed legs should. This support will also help you keep your back off the back of the chair. For regular meditation practice do not lean back in your chair.

The use of Magnetic Insulation

The whole path of Yoga is an attempt to harmonize with the way that life is made. We have already discussed that all of

The Hong-Sau Meditation Technique

life is energy and that energy creates a magnetic field. The earth itself is a powerful magnet. Yogis discovered that it is helpful to the practice of meditation if we insulate the body to some degree from the earth's magnetic field. If you are meditating on the floor just place a woolen blanket beneath you. When you sit on a chair the blanket should be placed on your seat and extend down beneath your feet. If you are inclined, you can also add a piece of silk over the wool blanket – this is said to be of additional benefit.

Head, Hand and Shoulder Positions

No matter how you are sitting, the head should be held with the chin tucked slightly in and parallel to the floor. The hands can be placed palms upward in any comfortable position on the thighs, but next to the juncture of the thigh and abdomen is best. The shoulder position is very key to keeping the upper spine straight. Most people slump their shoulders when sitting cross-legged – in fact many people slump their shoulders all the time!

The slumping of the shoulders crimps the flow of energy in the upper spine. In order to keep the upper spine straight the shoulders should be pulled back so that the shoulder blades are pulled together. When you do this you will find that your hands rest comfortably at the juncture of the thighs and abdomen. In the beginning this may seem like it is adding physical tension, but I can assure you that over time it will become the most natural and beneficial position.

It is like the correct hand position when you play a musical instrument. In the beginning it feels awkward, but over time you find that it is the best and most comfortable position for playing the instrument. It is the same with meditation. Just pull your shoulders back, feel how it straightens the upper spine

41

and then consciously relax the muscles in that position. Once you have learned to keep your shoulders back with relaxation you will find that you can move your arms to different positions without bending the upper spine.

Hong-Sau Meditation Technique

This technique is elegantly simple, yet the benefits from its practice are deeply profound. What we are trying to do is still the mind and experience the inner self without the storm of mental restlessness. In order to do this we are going to consciously link the mind to the breath. It is essential to understand that in this technique we DO NOT CONTROL THE BREATH. We allow the breath to flow in and flow out of its own accord. What we are going to do is watch the breath as it flows in and out. While we watch the breath we will use a mantra to help engage the mind fully.

Mantra Choices

It is recommended that you use the words Hong-Sau as the mantra. These Sanskrit words mean "I am He" or "I am Spirit". As I mentioned earlier, the Sanskrit language is vibrationally advantageous to our purpose. But…you may say it in English if you prefer. If you don't feel comfortable with the meaning of Hong-Sau then you can substitute the words "I am Peace", "I am Love" or "I am Joy". Remember, the mantra is not spoken with the voice, it is repeated mentally only.

The Breath and Mantra

When the breath comes in of its own accord you mentally say Hong (I am) and when the breath goes out of its own accord you mentally say Sau (He, Spirit, Peace, Love or Joy).

The Hong-Sau Meditation Technique

I should mention that Hong rhymes with Song and Sau sounds like Saw.

As you mentally say the mantra let it stretch or shrink in duration so that it equals the length of the inhalation or the exhalation.

It is important to find a specific place to watch the breath. You can watch the chest or lungs, the air as it flows in and out of the end of the nostrils or at the top of the nostril where the air enters the nasal cavity.

Unless you have breathing issues the air should be flowing of its own accord in and out of the nose. If you have to use your mouth to breath that isn't a problem, just focus your attention on wherever you are most aware of the breath. It doesn't matter if the breath is deep or shallow, just watch it as it flows.

Normal Practice

- Full Yogic Breath (Optional)

- Double Breathing with Tension 3 to 5 times.

- 12-12-12 Breathing (count according to your lung capacity, start with 6-6-6. Do 3 to 5 rounds).

- At the end of your last exhalation at the completion of 12-12-12 Breathing, begin your Hong-Sau practice by watching the breath without controlling it. Begin the mantra as the breath comes in all by itself.

- Mentally say Hong as the breath flows in and Sau as the breath flows out.

Meditation: The Science and Art of Stillness

- Practice Hong-Sau for 15 to 30 minutes.

- Sit in the silence after your practice. Enjoy the inner peace for 1/4 to 1/3 of the time you spend practicing the technique. So if you practice for 30 minutes sit in the silence for 10 minutes. You can always sit in the silence longer if you feel inclined.

Relaxed Practice

During the day you might find that you have a few free minutes. You can practice Hong-Sau casually without the preparation techniques but be sure that you keep intense inner focus. Do not practice Hong-Sau with a lackadaisical attitude. If you are alone try to sit as straight as you can. If you are in a public area then if you want to you can lean back in your chair like you are resting your eyes and begin your practice. (Remember, we do not lean back in our chair during regular meditation practice.)

- Start by taking two or three conscious deep breaths in the nose and out the mouth.

- At the end of the last deep exhalation start your practice of Hong-Sau.

- Practice for as long as seems appropriate in that situation.

- Try to sit in the silence for a period of time before you get up.

- Finish your practice by slowly inhaling through the nose and opening your eyes as you slowly exhale.

The Hong-Sau Meditation Technique

Practice Tips

* As you practice you will find at some point that your mind has wandered. Don't make a big deal out of it, just gently bring yourself back to focus on the breath and mantra.

* When thoughts try to appear in the background of your mind let them fly by rather than latching onto them.

* Work on focus first and then duration.

* In order to keep your shoulders back it will help if you concentrate on feeling that the upper spine is straight rather than thinking of the shoulder muscles themselves.

* It is not recommended to use the Hong-Sau mantra as a mantra alone. It isn't that it would hurt you in any way, but you are trying to train your mind. This mind body connection through the technique is very specific. It will help if you always associate the two together. There are many other mantras that can be used during the day for additional benefit if you want to add that to your practice.

* Practice Hong-Sau with an open heart. Meditation should always feel loving, joyful and expansive, not dry and mechanical.

* Paramhansa Yogananda recommended practicing Hong-Sau for up to two hours a day. Keep in mind that there are also other techniques to be used as well. If you

practice twice a day for 15 to 30 minutes you will see a dramatic difference in your life.

•   Regularity is the key to success. Even if you only sit for 1 minute try to do so twice a day. The idea that you will skip one day and do twice as much the next day rarely works. At the same time, it usually doesn't help to feel guilty about what you don't do, just concentrate on the good things that you are doing.

•   While we want to stay focused, it is essential that we stay relaxed. So check yourself occasionally and consciously relax and release any mental or physical tensions that you notice.

•   If you have trouble staying focused on the mantra for an extended period of time try this idea. Do one mantra for 5 minutes and then switch to another mantra variation for 5 minutes. The new mantra will freshen your efforts. Just keep in mind that the goal is to use only one mantra for your full Hong-Sau session.

•   As your practice deepens, don't just watch the breath, be the breath.

•   When you get up from meditation practice try to hold onto the inner calmness for as long as you can.

Chapter 6
Meditation Practice

While it is true that you can meditate anytime, anywhere, most often your regular meditation practice will take place at home. Here are some ideas that can help you to increase both your comfort and your success. Keep in mind that meditation practice is not about following a rigid set of rules. As you gain in experience you will intuitively discover how to mix and match all of these issues into a whole that works best for you.

Meditation Space

It is very helpful if you create a space where you only meditate. You can use a spare room, a closet or a screened off portion of your bedroom. The key here is that the only use for this space is meditation – so your bed wouldn't be a good idea, since you usually sleep there. Over time you will build both subconscious and superconscious associations that will help your efforts. It is important that you won't be disturbed in this space while you are meditating.

The ability for the space to be dark can be helpful, but it is not required – though flashing lights coming in a window wouldn't be such a great idea! While it isn't usually a problem,

Meditation: The Science and Art of Stillness

keep in mind that you want sufficient fresh air in the space so that it doesn't cause you to feel like sleeping.

Keeping the space a little cooler, so that you might need a light shawl for comfort is better than keeping the room too warm - which also encourages drowsiness.

Meditation Seat

Your asan (seat for meditation) should be used only for meditation. So if you use a pillow, blanket, shawl, kneeling bench or chair, it should stay in your meditation space so that it is not used by others. Do not share your meditation seat with others, as you are building an energetic momentum that will be disturbed by their energy – of course visiting saints are an exception to this guideline! There might be times when you want to sit in your meditation room with a baby or very small child. In this case they will be in your lap or very close to you - your regular meditation sessions should not be linked to childcare - otherwise visitors to your meditation space should have their own seat.

Direction

Yogis say that it is best to face east when meditating. North would be the second choice. After that it doesn't matter.

Sound

Noise pollution is a real challenge. This is one of the reasons yogis like caves. While a soundproof room would be ideal, most people won't have this as an option. Through practice you will be able to meditate even in a noisy place. You may want to experiment with noise reduction headphones like they use around airplanes and/or soft earplugs.

Focus Point

Many people like to use an altar for the focusing of their meditation and devotional efforts. This can range from a simple candle to elaborately decorated pictures and statues. This is a completely personal choice and is not in any way required. Keep in mind that candles and incense use up oxygen, so be sure the space is well ventilated if you use these.

When to Meditate

The most common times for meditation are after getting up in the morning before starting the day and in the evening before going to sleep. The key is to find at least two times during the day that you can practice regularly. Creating the habit of meditating at the same time and place is very beneficial. If you can add a short meditation around lunchtime, that would of extra benefit.

In India it is said that those times when nature is in transition - sunrise, noon, sunset and midnight – are the best times for meditation. If you can somehow coordinate with these rhythms of nature it is helpful. But don't forget…anytime is a good time to meditate!

Duration

The most basic meditation practice should be 15 to 30 minutes. Of course in the beginning some people will feel like five minutes is an eternity. It is better to meditate 5 to 15 minutes with focus then thirty minutes with your mind wandering. There are times though, when restlessness has taken hold of you, that you should just make yourself sit there for a period of time. Once the body/mind realizes you mean business, they will give up their rebellion.

Meditation: The Science and Art of Stillness

In the beginning the mind and body will rebel. They are used to constant stimulus and may complain with thoughts and itches that need immediate attention. The key to adding length in meditation is depth of focus. If you are really concentrated on the breath and mantra you will lose track of time.

In the beginning set yourself a minimum, even if it is just 1 to 5 minutes. Sincerity of effort and regular practice will lead to a natural lengthening of your ability to inwardly concentrate.

Devotion

While meditation doesn't require devotion to a specific religion or spiritual form, your efforts will be greatly enhanced if you include not only an open heart but an active heart. Let me explain.

The water pipes in a house have water in them. We all have love in our hearts. That love is dormant when it just sits inside us. It is made manifest, just like water coming from a faucet, when we allow it to flow through us.

When we meditate we are trying to create and harmonize with a focused flow of energy. During successful concentration it will feel like your awareness is constantly flowing towards the object of concentration. When we are consciously connected to and absorbed into this flow we will be meditating well.

Devotion should not be confused with emotion. You don't need to start crying in order to feel the energy of your heart. In fact, most of the time crying is a big distraction and often a sign of restless emotion instead of devotion. We are not seeking an emotional catharsis. You don't even have to call it love.

Try this experiment.

Close your eyes. Take two deep breaths and consciously relax your body and mind. Put your awareness at the point near your heart - this is called the Anahat Chakra or heart center - where you feel most connected to the feeling of love. When you find that point use your mind to consciously switch on the love in your heart. As you mentally flip the switch imagine that love is radiating out from your heart center in all directions like a miniature sun. Sit for a few minutes and let this love shine through your body and mind out into the world.

In order to help awaken the energy flowing through the heart center many people use devotional chanting. This is a whole subject unto itself which would be a distraction at this point. Let me just say that this is a helpful practice with this caveat: when using devotional chanting do not whip up the emotions. Open your heart but stay calm. The goal isn't to enjoy the music or get emotionally excited, but to use the music as a focal point to go through it to stillness. This is what we are doing in a more direct way when we meditate.

If you can practice meditation with your heart center consciously open it will add a whole new dimension to your practice.

Routine

As you grow in experience you will find a routine that feels comfortable to you. Here is a rough guideline that will give you a sense of direction with your practice. Feel free to delete any part of this list that doesn't fit your needs or approach.

Meditation: The Science and Art of Stillness

- Prayer – this can be specific to your path or a general bowing of the mind and heart in humility and appreciation for life.

- Full Yogic Breath – 3 to 7 times.

- Yoga Postures – As you have time and interest.

- Devotional Chanting – You can include chanting before or after meditation as you feel inclined.

- Energization – Double breathing with tension. If you know more of Yogananda's Energization Exercises do them before practicing the Full Yogic Breath.

- Pranayama – Practice 12-12-12 Breathing 3 to 7 times according to your lung capacity.

- Meditation – Practice Hong-Sau Meditation Technique for 15 to 30 minutes.

- Sit in the Silence – Sit calmly with an open heart in the inner stillness.

- If you have questions or challenges in life this is the time to inwardly present them to God/the Universe as you feel inclined.

- Sit in the Silence – Just in case you get a response!

- Pray for others – It has been scientifically proven that prayer works. This is a great time to ask God/the Universe to bless others.

•   Give Thanks – Take a moment of prayer or simple appreciation for life itself

As I said, you can mix and match these components in any way that you like. You don't have to do all this at every session unless you have the time and inclination. This is just to give you a sense of how many people put this all together. Refer to the Regular Practice and Relaxed Practice headings in the last chapter to remind yourself of the most basic ways to practice the Hong-Sau Meditation Technique.

Chapter 7
The Meditation Lifestyle

The teachings of Yoga do not provide a long "Do this and Do not do that!" list of rules. Yoga provides a system for evaluating how life affects us and techniques for self-realization that work in concert with that knowledge. This way we can make choices according to the unique circumstances of our own lives.

Top class athletes will easily understand when arriving at training camp that a complete regimen includes both things we do and things we do not do. Just like dieting, when you want to lose weight there are the foods you eat and the foods you do not eat. It is the same when we look at the lifestyle that is most beneficial for meditation.

In Yoga, the system for doing this is called the Gunas (qualities). The Gunas represent directions of consciousness.

Expanding and Contracting Consciousness

Most people live in what is described as Ego consciousness. We believe that we are a body and mind. Some people also believe we are Spirit (soul) but they aren't exactly sure what that means. Let me paint a very simplified picture.

Meditation: The Science and Art of Stillness

All of life is an infinite ocean. Each of us are like waves on that ocean. The wave is the soul and the froth around the wave is the ego. As a wave we feel separate from all other waves, but as a part of the ocean we are actually still one with all of life.

As we expand our consciousness we begin to remember - Smriti (Divine memory) - our reality as part of the ocean. When we identify more with ourselves as the froth of the wave we are living in contracted consciousness - which is subject to the pleasure and pain storms of life. As we meditate we are seeking to connect to and be ever more aware of the ocean of consciousness.

The Three Gunas

The three Gunas are: Sattwa (elevating or expanding), Rajas (activating) and Tamas (downward pulling or contracting). Like the green, yellow, red, colors on a traffic signal the three Gunas can keep us from crashing into the pitfalls of ego consciousness.

Sattwa Guna

Anything that we do in life that expands and elevates our consciousness is said to be Sattwa or Sattvic (In Sanskrit the actual sound of v and w is between the v and w sounds of English, so the word can be spelled with a v or w interchangeably). To all things Sattwa we give the green light. The association with these qualities leads to happiness. Here are some examples of Sattvic qualities.

- Beautiful places

- Compassion

- Cheerfulness

- Beautiful flowers and their scents

- Peace

- Love

- Cleanliness of body and mind

- Food vital with life force

- The inclination to help others

Raja Guna

Rajasic qualities are activating. To them we give the yellow light. This is a warning that activating energies can go in an elevating expanding direction or toward a Tamasic downward pulling contracting direction. High energy in itself is beneficial, but the misdirection of that energy can lead to problems.

- **Music** - Inherently activating but it can be Sattvic if it takes you toward stillness or Tamasic if it takes you towards body/emotion awareness. No matter what music you listen to, if you listen all the time it will cause restlessness in the mind.

- **Sports** - Activating. Hatha Yoga points toward Sattwa. Sports that encourage anger or violence point toward Tamas. The martial arts can be positive when used for self-development and negative when used to harm others. Sports that encourage cooperation are beneficial in that aspect. Dancing a waltz or ballet can lean toward expanding, while slam dancing would be contracting.

- **Television, Movies and Reading Material** - Movies and Television are by their nature Rajasic. Most people can tell if what they watch is uplifting, active but neutral or representative of negative ideas and energies. Books and magazines as a medium are less Rajasic, but they are still powerful communicators of not only ideas, but vibrations.

Tama Guna

Tamasic qualities, are contractive downward pulling qualities. To these we give the red STOP signal. For they inevitably lead to suffering.

- Laziness

- A filthy dwelling

- Food that is over cooked or not fresh

- Selfishness

- Places were evil deeds have been committed

- Jealousy or vengefulness

- Swearing

All of life is a mixture of these three qualities. Even in the most elevating place there will be a bug. In the darkest war there are acts of heroism. The point of this isn't to look at everything and judge it, but to recognize how we are affected by the world around us and consciously choose that which will lead to happiness. The more sensitive we become inwardly the more clearly we can read the energy qualities of life around us.

The Meditation Lifestyle

It is important to understand that whether you are seeking stress reduction or self-realization, this is about a whole lifestyle and not just a meditation shot in the arm. The more we meditate the more aware we will become of the subtle influence that life around us has on our inner peace. When you go to a restaurant you will notice if it is calm, warm and friendly, or overcrowded with noise and negative attitudes. You may also notice if the food is light and vibrant with fresh energy or if it is overcooked, heavy and lifeless. These are things that some people never notice, but as you meditate more you will recognize these qualities of energy for what they are and begin to change your life accordingly.

Of course there is a time and a place for extremes. You may choose to go to an amusement park or the county fair where excitement and stimulation are the whole point. Have a good time! Just don't be fooled into thinking that this type of stimulation is the same as happiness.

If you live a generally calm lifestyle you can easily fit in days of excitement without losing your inner balance. But if you live everyday in the fast lane and don't balance it with peaceful activities, you will find that restlessness, insomnia and depression are going to take up residence in your life.

Diet for Meditation

We use the guidelines of the Gunas to choose our food as well. Along with nutrient content we need to recognize that food has vibrational content as well. Sattvic foods - like fruits, nuts, fresh vegetables, sprouts, yogurt and tofu - help us to feel light and energetic. Rajasic foods - sugar, carbohydrates, proteins and spices - can lead to a restless and/or sluggish body/mind, or to a healthy body/mind that is strong and fit. Tamasic

Meditation: The Science and Art of Stillness

foods - over processed food, food with no life force and food cooked by people with negative attitudes - lead to slothfulness, excessive body consciousness and disease.

Taking conscious control of your diet can lead to dramatic improvements in mental and physical well-being, but a healthy diet won't by itself lead to peace and eventually self-realization.

For general purposes it is recommended that you establish a basic vegetarian diet and then forget about it. If you do eat meat then try to stick with fish, and then poultry, which are considered the better choices. If you have special health needs and/or a strong interest in this subject there are many good books available about vegetarian nutrition and cooking styles.

The Canvas of Your Life

Each of us is the artist that creates the picture that will represent our life. It doesn't matter what happens to us, pleasant or unpleasant, we are the ones that get to choose how we will react. Some of the greatest lives have come from great suffering and some of the worst have come from people who had every advantage. Life isn't so much about what happens to us, but the qualities of energy that flow through us. The ideas that we are covering will give you a larger color palette to work with and brushes that can make new and different strokes for wide reaching effects. I encourage you to explore the application of new subtle colors in your life that will yield deeply rewarding results.

Life is challenging. If it weren't it wouldn't be very interesting. By using the filter of the Gunas we can mix and match the components of our lives in a way that will establish the center of our being in a strong connection to inner happiness. Then as life flows around us we will have the strength, courage and peace of mind to step forward with confidence. This approach is anchored in our ability to connect to life from the inside out instead of living from the outside in. Your meditation practice, when supported by conscious positive choices, will lead you to inner and outer success.

Chapter 8
9 Keys
to Success
in Meditation

Mentors

No matter how we are trying to improve ourselves, the help of a mentor is extremely beneficial. People are notoriously bad at self-evaluation; we are simply too close to ourselves to have a clear perspective. And of course, without the development of self-honesty, introspection is flawed from the very beginning. As I previously mentioned, most often we just don't have the experience to know exactly how to help ourselves.

Over time, meditation will help us to introspect with more clarity, but in the beginning and for a long time to come, the guidance of an experienced meditator who practices the same technique you practice is immensely beneficial. The willingness to receive instruction and inspiration from others is also a part of freeing ourselves from ego consciousness. Humility is a very Satvic quality.

Another aspect to this is the process of absorption. Mentors not only provide intellectual information but they transmit vibrational content that we take in not only consciously, but subconsciously and superconsciously.

Meditation: The Science and Art of Stillness
The Test of Your Resolve

No matter what you try to accomplish in this life the universe will try to test your resolve. Meditation is no different. The mind will come up with many reasons to delay or put off practicing – You are too tired! You are too busy, you don't have time! Take a break! Have some fun! Relax! Friends will invite you to do other activities. They may try to convince you that meditation is bad or that you should try their style. It doesn't really matter the intentions, which are often good intentions, 99 times out of 100 at that moment they represent the negative flow of life that is trying to keep us from experiencing inner freedom. Developing the regular habit of meditation will help you in this regard, but you are never really safe until you are fully inwardly free.

Sitting Still

Learning to sit absolutely still during meditation is essential. If your body is fidgeting your mind will never become calm. In fact, a restless body is a reflection of a restless mind. Once you get settled into a comfortable position, just don't move. If you can force yourself to sit absolutely still for 5 minutes, you can relatively easily extend that amount of time to 30 minutes or an hour.

Often when you sit to meditate you will notice an itch and reach to scratch the offending spot. Then you will find that an incredible number of places on your body will suddenly demand to be scratched, one after another. The amazing thing is that once you have ignored them for about 30 seconds, they will all go away!

When you become sufficiently absorbed in the practice of meditation the body and time will cease to concern you.

9 Keys to Success in Meditation

How to Move without Disturbing your Meditation

Even after you have learned to sit still, you will find that during extended periods of meditation you may need to briefly move the body. It is possible to take care of these needs with a minimum of disturbance. Here are some ideas.

- If you really have to scratch something - Do it quickly and then don't respond to any of the new itches that will pop up to see if they can get your attention.

- If a limb falls to sleep - Move it just enough to get the blood flowing again. If you move it too far or shake it you will get that tingling sensation that you probably won't be able to fully ignore. Once the blood has returned to the limb, place it calmly into a new position and forget about it.

- Move from sitting on the floor to sitting in a chair - Do so in a calm flowing motion so that you minimize pulling your mind out into the body. Once in the seat settle yourself as quickly as possible into not moving.

- Meditation Platform - Consider making a piano bench style meditation seat that has enough room on top so that you can sit cross-legged or with your feet on the floor. This way you can easily change positions without too much distraction.

Regular Meditation

I have already mentioned the need for regular meditation but it is important enough to be worth mentioning again. Like many things in life, the more we do it the better we get at it. Simply put: The more you meditate the more you will

Meditation: The Science and Art of Stillness

want to meditate; the less you meditate the less you will want to meditate.

Group Meditation

While meditation is most often a solitary practice, attending group meditations on any kind of regular basis is very helpful. The group energy will give support to your efforts. It will sometimes give feedback about how you are doing. More often than you might think it will propel you to inner depths that are more difficult to achieve on your own. You also serve others when you add your sincere efforts to theirs.

Interaction with other people who meditate can also be helpful to the rest of your life. Other meditators are more likely to be in harmony with your lifestyle and life goals. Social interaction with other like-minded people will enhance the totality of your life.

No matter what you choose to do in life it is helpful if you "hang out" with those who are good at what you want to do. They will inspire you and their positive life energy will spill over into your own life.

During the Day

You can support your meditation practice by trying some of these ideas.

- Make time to take a few minutes for Relaxed Practice of the Hong-Sau technique.

- Take a 30 second peace break – Close your eyes and take two deep conscious breaths and mentally remember the calm feeling that you have in meditation.

- Make a practice, as much as possible, of only listening to calming, uplifting music.

- Eat foods that don't bog you down.

- Don't be drawn into arguments.

- Practice reacting to negative situations with conscious calmness.

- Work with an attitude of joy and service to others.

The Spiritual Eye

The place of positive polarity in the magnetic spine is a point just between and slightly above the eyebrows. This energy center has been called the third eye, the single eye, the star of the east, the Christ center, the Ajna chakra and probably many more names. No matter what you call it, something is definitely going on there! It is so important that Paramhansa Yogananda said, "Live from the spiritual eye, come down to eat and talk as necessary, then withdraw back to the spiritual eye."

Over time with the practice of meditation you will become aware of this energy center in just the same way that you are aware of the heart center. This is not an issue of belief, it is an actual experience. The heart connected to the spiritual eye is the portal to higher consciousness.

Here are some ideas for deepening your awareness of this center:

- Place the forefinger of your right hand about one inch above the point where your eyebrows meet. Then close your eyes and gently look up at that point. Do not strain your eyes. It is not beneficial to make yourself cross-eyed.

- Over time you will feel energy flowing to this point during meditation. Relax into the flow of the energy rather than actually trying to see something. If you do see something, the more relaxed you stay the clearer it will become. The key is to focus without tension.

- You may at some point feel the gathering of energy at this point. This is a positive sign. Just stay relaxed and allow the sensation to flow towards the spiritual eye.

- You may see light. When seen clearly the spiritual eye is blue, surrounded by a gold circle and centered with a white 5 pointed star. This is a universal experience, you don't have to imagine it, one day it will just happen.

- Your energy spine is just in front of the physical spine in the center of the body. Experiment by centering your awareness in your heart center and relaxing into its wellspring of love. Then mentally direct your feeling of love up the spine and out the spiritual eye. Feel, like water through a hose, that your love is flowing up the spine and through the spiritual eye.

- The more aware you are of energy rising in your spine from the base to the spiritual eye, the better. When you feel this energy, let it flow up the spine and out through the spiritual eye.

- Take all of your life experiences into the spine and

then direct them up and through the spiritual eye. When you make a habit of this it will help you to be more aware of life's underlying energies and help free you from being negatively affected by unwanted influences.

- If your breath pauses during the practice of the Hong-Sau technique, stay relaxed and gently look up into the spiritual eye.

Present Everything to the Universe

Whatever your need is in life, whether it is help with meditation, finding a mentor or dealing with any challenge in life; offer it up in the peace after meditation. You don't need to believe in God, you can simply offer whatever it is to the invisible universe. Of course if you do believe in God then participate in that belief by presenting these issues up for guidance/resolution.

As I mentioned, no matter your religious or non religious background, if you act like the universe is your friend and create an inner dialogue – which means talking and listening - you will find in uncanny ways that the universe responds. Many people do this all the time and find that it works so powerfully that they can't quite believe it, even though they have experienced it, so they call it all coincidence. All I can say is, try it, you will like it!

Chapter 9
Deeper
Techniques
of Meditation

The ideas and techniques that we have explored so far are sufficient in a meaningful way to guide you in experiencing for yourself the value of meditation. If you don't practice meditation, your interest will fade away. With diligent practice you will experience inner peace and improved life balance. Your success may motivate you to deepen your meditation practice. Here are some ways that you can move forward.

Kriya Yoga

The *Hong-Sau Technique* is one of four main techniques that Paramhansa Yogananda taught. I have already mentioned the *Energization Exercises* of which we learned the first of a series of 39 exercises. Yogananda also taught the *Aum Meditation Technique* and the most advanced technique, *Kriya Yoga*. The *Energization Exercises* - which take about 15 minutes to complete - use conscious will to direct life force to all of the body parts for the recharging of the body and mind. The *Hong-Sau Technique* guides us in learning to concentrate the mind inwardly. The *Aum Meditation Technique* helps us to focus our concentration on the inner sounds and waves of peace that are at the core of the universe. The *Kriya Yoga* meditation technique utilizes the skills learned in the previous techniques and works directly with the life force in the spine to accelerate dramatically the process of self-realization. The practice of these techniques leads to deeper and deeper experiences of universal peace, love and joy.

All of these techniques, when applied with a lifestyle that supports their purpose, comprise the main components necessary for the achievement of Self-Realization – the conscious knowing in body, mind and spirit that you are the ocean of infinite consciousness and not only the wave of ego.

These techniques are taught all around the world and are offered to people of all races and nations regardless of their religious affiliation – or lack thereof. Again, I recommend that you learn them from an experienced practitioner. Feel free to contact me through the publisher for more information about these techniques.

Silence

The practice of consciously not speaking is very powerful. Unless you have tried this you won't realize how much energy it takes to talk. The first time you keep silence you will have to fight the urge to speak. You may even speak accidently until your mind fully accepts the idea. It is not only the act of speaking that takes energy, but all of the thinking that goes into deciding what to say. It is very calming to the mind to turn off the expenditure of this often restless and unnecessary effort.

Experiment with different lengths of time. You can start by consciously not speaking for five minutes, an hour or a day. If you link this to personal seclusion (which is discussed on the next page) it is very powerful. Mahatma Gandhi regularly kept silence one day a week. If he needed to communicate with someone on that day he would write them a note. There is a well known picture of Gandhi in *Autobiography of a Yogi* in which Yogananda is reading a note Gandhi wrote requesting initiation into *Kriya Yoga*.

Some yogis in the recognition of the value of silence take a vow never to speak. I am not suggesting that this is even necessary for self-realization, but I offer these ideas in the hope that you will experiment with the practice.

Fasting

This practice isn't for everyone, but it is effective if not overdone. Just in the same way the mind is calmed by not speaking, the whole body is given a chance to rejuvenate when we stop requiring it to digest food for a period of time. You should consider your current state of health before fasting. I would suggest trying one day as an experiment. Some people prefer to try drinking fruit juices or tea rather than just water on their first effort to fast – no matter what you try, stay hydrated. It is essential to educate yourself on the subject of fasting before trying any period longer then a day.

Personal Seclusion

The practice of seclusion can be done at a retreat facility or at home. The key is to withdraw from daily life as completely as possible and focus your full attention on your inner life. This normally includes extended periods of meditation, silence, reduced eating - if not fasting - reading only highly uplifting material, light exercise and/or yoga postures. This means no phone, no TV/Video – unless you are practicing with a Hatha Yoga DVD or watching a spiritual discourse, computer only for writing a journal - not for web surfing or social/work e-mail, music only if it is very calming and uplifting.

Meditation: The Science and Art of Stillness

In seclusion we can really take leaps forward in our meditation progress. I highly recommend it.

Retreat

Meditation retreats offer programs that have many different themes along with meditation. You can take courses or you can create your own schedule. Some retreats offer support for serious personal seclusion and others offer lots of activities. Be sure to check carefully into the program you are considering. As I have said, the word meditation doesn't mean the same thing to everyone. Sometimes people say they meditate and it means five minutes of soft music. Other groups may meditate for longer then you feel comfortable. So be sure the retreat you select has the type of atmosphere and practices that are in harmony with your needs. It is additionally beneficial to go to a place that practices the same techniques that you are practicing.

Devotion

The cultivation of what Swami Sri Yukteswar described as "the natural love of the heart" is essential for serious spiritual practices. Without the cultivation of this love Sri Yukteswar said, "You can't take one step on the spiritual path."

We talked briefly about devotional chanting. Yogananda went so far as to say, "Chanting is half the battle." Let's face it; singing is a lot easier than meditation. If you use devotional chants they will fill your mind and heart with loving and expanding thoughts and vibrations. Just don't over emotionalize them and be sure to take them into the silence.

Deeper techniques of Meditation

Prayer

The subject of prayer is worth revisiting. This is a powerful tool. If you doubt that God/the Universe is participant in your life than simply strike up an inner conversation and see what happens. You don't need to be part of a religion, in fact sometimes that keeps people from feeling free to say what they really feel and believe in the responses that they receive. People have an incredible number of misconceptions about God and spirituality. Yoga says: Explore for yourself. Suspend doubt for a while and see what happens, what do you have to lose?

Prayer can be used to express your feelings, ask a question and/or send positive energy to others. Be sure to connect the silence you feel after meditation to your prayer. Emotional expressions are useful at times, but calm silence is the place to feel a response.

Spiritual Community

Finding your spiritual family is one of the greatest supports there is for meditation and a great way to live. Surrounding yourself with other like-minded people is the smartest thing you can do no matter what you are trying to accomplish. There are rural and urban spiritual communities all around the world and many of them are thriving. If this strikes a bell in you, do some research while you invite God/the Universe to participate and guide you in finding just the right group.

Chapter 10
The Fruits
of Meditation

While most people can see how closing your eyes for a few minutes might be peaceful, since the eyes are closed during a good nap, the idea of closing your eyes and discovering the essence of all life might seem farfetched and awaken serious doubt. But we have not wandered in the desert of speculation. Our journey together has covered specific techniques and guidelines.

Here are some of the basic results that millions of meditators have experienced. Keep in mind that each person's mix of natural ability and clarity of application will differ; so we can't expect everyone to experience the same thing at the same time according to how many days they have been meditating.

If you don't have any of these experiences you should consider the possibility that you are not following the procedures as they have been described. While it isn't all that common, it is possible you have a health issue that is compromising your efforts in some way. For example: Some prescription drugs cause agitation of the mind. If you are experiencing this you might want to discuss it with your physician. Or if you are so restless that you can't sit still at all, it will take you longer to

Meditation: The Science and Art of Stillness

experience calmness. For either of these two situations I would suggest that the practice of Ananda style Hatha Yoga before meditation is imperative.

By far, the number one reason people don't achieve the results they seek is that they simply don't practice regularly.

Common Meditation Experiences

• Calmness – You should feel this during meditation, but often the depth of your calmness strikes you when you get up from your meditation and start interacting with the world.

• Peace – This is different than calmness. Calmness is a little distant; peace is a close feeling of well-being.

• Bliss - This takes some time to achieve, but it is an upwelling of joy that rises in the spine to the spiritual eye. The first time you feel it, you will know exactly what it is.

• Inner Sounds - Some people hear various sounds that are connected to Aum - the inner sound of the universe. Whatever you hear, experiment with relaxing into it and see if it intensifies. The most important thing about the sounds is that they should be accompanied with a feeling of calmness; embrace the calmness.

• Inner Light – I mentioned the spiritual eye. Some people see the spiritual eye early in their practice and others not for years. It isn't something to be concerned about, but if it happens you now know what it is. Some people see different colors. This is not a goal. Inner calmness and focus are more important than seeing anything.

• Don't Seek Flashy Experiences – I know they sound cool, but once you get off on this track they are very likely to be imagination. Unless they are connected to deep feelings of peace, calmness and/or bliss, they are most commonly a distraction.

Life Changes

• More aware of how things feel around you.

• More sensitive to avoiding negative situations.

• More aware of the needs of others than your own.

• More objective when evaluating yourself.

• More contentment while continuing to seek self improvement.

• More able to come up with positive solutions to life challenges.

• Greater willingness to admit mistakes without excessive guilt.

• Increased creativity.

• Less inclined toward anger.

• Less inclined toward excessive outward stimulation.

• Able to feel that you are living in the positive flow for your life.

• Generally happier!

Meditation: The Science and Art of Stillness

There is no more central way to improve the quality of our lives than by a regular practice of meditation. Meditation reaches into the essence of our being and cleans house while leaving a pleasant aroma of good feeling. Through your meditation practice you will find that every life experience can be turned into an opportunity for greater happiness.

My humble prayer is that your efforts in meditation may be blessed with success.

Namaste.

Support for your Meditation Practice
You may contact the author with questions via e-mail through the publisher's website.

www.FruitgardenPublishing.com

More books
by Lawrence Vijay Girard
(Nayaswami Vijay)

Way of the Positive Flow

Positive Flow Parenting

Flowing in the Workplace:
A Guide to Personal and
Professional Success

Doorway to a New Lifetime:
Childbirth from a Spiritual View

The Journey of Discipleship
Book 1 - Traveling with Swamiji

The Adventures of
Harry Fruitgarden
Series
Book #1 - What's it All About?
Book #2 - Who Would Have Guessed?

Ask us about
Positive Flow Seminars
with Lawrence Vijay Girard
(Nayaswami Vijay)

www.FruitgardenPublishing.com

www.ingramcontent.com/pod-product-compliance
Lightning Source LLC
Chambersburg PA
CBHW071017040426
42443CB00007B/822